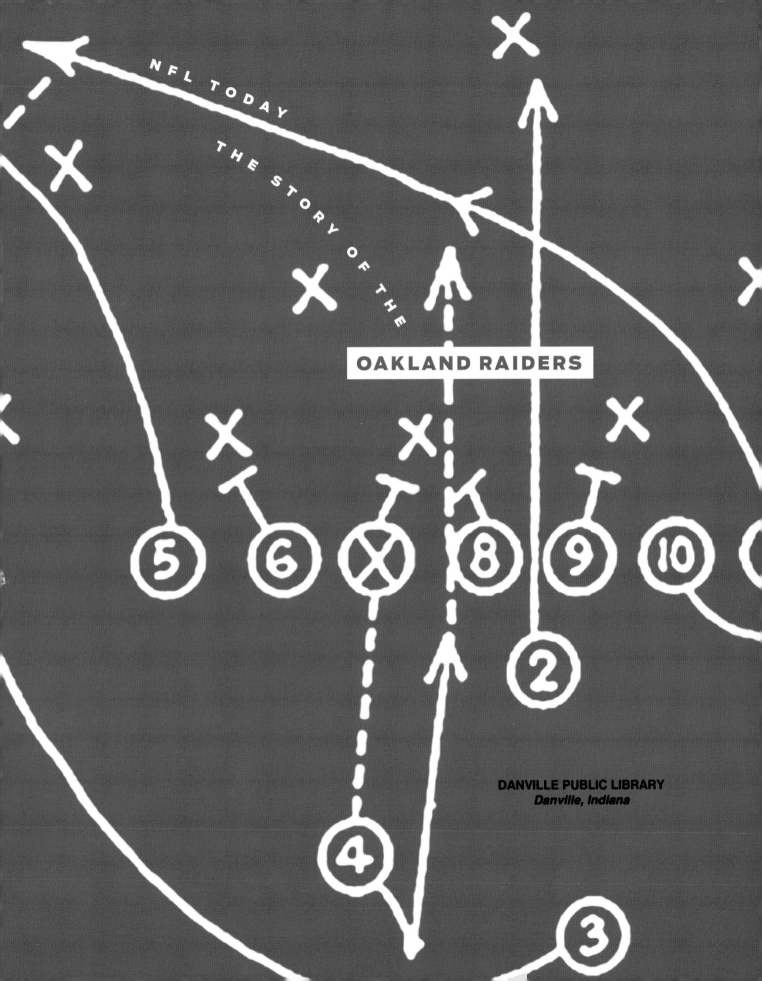

NFL TODAY

THE STORY OF THE

OAKLAND RAIDERS

NFL TODAY

THE STORY OF THE OAKLAND RAIDERS

NATE FRISCH

CREATIVE EDUCATION

PUBLISHED BY CREATIVE EDUCATION
P.O. BOX 227, MANKATO, MINNESOTA 56002
CREATIVE EDUCATION IS AN IMPRINT OF THE CREATIVE COMPANY
WWW.THECREATIVECOMPANY.US

DESIGN AND PRODUCTION BY BLUE DESIGN
ART DIRECTION BY RITA MARSHALL
PRINTED IN THE UNITED STATES OF AMERICA

PHOTOGRAPHS BY CORBIS (BETTMANN), GETTY
IMAGES (BRIAN BAHR, B. BENNETT, MORRIS BERMAN/
NFL, BERNSTEIN ASSOCIATES, MATT CAMPBELL/
AFP, STEPHEN DUNN, JOHN ELK III, JAMES FLORES/
NFL PHOTOS, FOCUS ON SPORT, GRANT HALVERSON,
NEIL LEIFER/SPORTS ILLUSTRATED, GEORGE LONG/
NFL, JOHN G. MABANGLO/AFP, TAKASHI MAKITA/
NFL, AL MESSERSCHMIDT/NFL, RONALD C. MODRA/
SPORTS IMAGERY, NFL, MIKE POWELL, JOE ROBBINS,
EZRA SHAW, THOMAS B. SHEN, PAUL SPINELLI, JAMIE
SQUIRE, RICK STEWART/ALLSPORT, KEVIN TERRELL,
GREG TROTT, MICHAEL ZAGARIS)

LIBRARY OF CONGRESS CATALOGING-IN-PUBLICATION DATA
FRISCH, NATE.
THE STORY OF THE OAKLAND RAIDERS / BY NATE FRISCH.
P. CM. — (NFL TODAY)
INCLUDES INDEX.
SUMMARY: THE HISTORY OF THE NATIONAL FOOTBALL LEAGUE'S
OAKLAND RAIDERS, SURVEYING THE FRANCHISE'S BIGGEST
STARS AND MOST MEMORABLE MOMENTS FROM ITS INAUGURAL
SEASON IN 1960 TO TODAY.
ISBN 978-1-60818-314-2
1. OAKLAND RAIDERS (FOOTBALL TEAM)—HISTORY—JUVENILE
LITERATURE. I. TITLE.

GV956.O24F76 2013
796.332'640979466—DC23   2012033813

FIRST EDITION
9 8 7 6 5 4 3 2 1

COVER AND PAGE 2: RUNNING BACK DARREN MCFADDEN
PAGES 4–5: WIDE RECEIVER FRED BILETNIKOFF
PAGE 6: GUARD GENE UPSHAW

TABLE OF CONTENTS

SIDELINE STORIES

MEET THE RAIDERS

OAKLAND IS THE BUSIEST PORT ON SAN FRANCISCO BAY

Renegade Roots

The city of Oakland lies along the San Francisco Bay in California. In decades long past, the West Coast city was the site of many economic activities, including logging and agriculture, but it was the California Gold Rush that officially put the city on the map in 1852. In more modern times, Oakland has established itself as a major shipping port. Beginning around the 1960s, the city also earned an undesirable reputation for a higher-than-average rate of crime and riots. Today, sitting in the shadow of its more glamorous "sister city," San Francisco, Oakland still maintains something of a rebellious image.

Before 1960, Oakland did not have any major professional sports teams, and, were it not for a twist of fate, things might have stayed that way. The city hadn't really even expressed much interest in hosting a football team. Oakland had no stadium, and San Francisco was already home to the 49ers of the National Football League (NFL). In 1960, the American Football League (AFL) was created to compete with the NFL. Of

BEN DAVIDSON WAS ONE OF THE FACES OF THE 1960s RAIDERS

Jim Otto

CENTER / RAIDERS SEASONS: 1960–74 / HEIGHT: 6-FOOT-2 / WEIGHT: 255 POUNDS

Wearing number 00 wasn't Jim Otto's only notable distinction as a player. For 10 years—the entire existence of the AFL—Otto was voted All-AFL as the best center in the league every season. "He loved to win," said Oakland quarterback George Blanda. "He led by example and he set the tempo. He gave the Raiders an image of hard discipline, hard work, and hard-nosed football." As a testament to this image, Otto played through many injuries. During a 1972 preseason game against the Buffalo Bills, he tore five ligaments in his right leg on the same play. The team doctor said Otto's season was over, and likely his career, too. But Otto not only played in the season opener three weeks later, he also made the 1972 Pro Bowl. In Otto's mind, the price he paid in pain was worth it. "I was paid to play football, not hang out in the training room," he said. "That will, that drive to continue playing was derived from self-motivation." After retiring as a player, Otto remained with the team as a member of owner Al Davis's management staff.

the AFL's original eight teams, Oakland was the last to be added, and then only after other cities had declined to host a team. As many franchises do, Oakland asked local fans to submit suggestions for the team's name, and "Raiders" was chosen. The name was initially meant to imply pirates, but it could also describe other renegades or outlaws. As time went on, Oakland fans and players would seem to embrace the latter meaning.

The Raiders were desperate from the start. Since Oakland was the last team to get an AFL franchise, its quickly assembled ownership group didn't have a lot of time or money to work with. The Raiders wore secondhand uniforms and helmets without logos, and their home field wasn't even in Oakland— they shared Kezar Stadium with the 49ers in San Francisco. Team owner Chet Soda also had a difficult time signing players, so head coach Eddie Erdelatz had to scrounge for talent. Although he found some in the form of players such as quarterback Tom Flores and halfback Wayne Crow, the young Raiders went a collective 9–33 from 1960 to 1962. The future looked bleak, but Oakland had at least one star around whom it could build: center Jim Otto.

Otto was a terrific player and a steady leader whom many football fans still remember for his unusual jersey number: 00. Some NFL players and experts wondered why such a talented player would sign on with a team in the AFL, a league most people considered to be inferior to the NFL. "I could make some NFL clubs, I know," Otto said. "But it's more of an honor and distinction to be an original member of a brand-new league."

Things improved in 1963 when Al Davis, a young coach from San Diego, took over as Oakland's head coach and general manager. Davis brought big ideas and a new energy level to the young squad. One of his first goals was to build an intimidating team image that reflected the city's outsider status. He did this by outfitting his players in new uniforms of silver and black and adding a tough-looking helmet logo. "Because of Oakland's image, and the type of team image Al wanted to build, the bond was natural for us," fullback Mark van Eeghen said.

Davis instructed his team to play with two *Ps*: pride and poise. "Poise is the secret," he announced. "No matter what the scoreboard says, keep your poise." With Davis running the operation, the 1963 Raiders jumped to 10–4, and he was named the AFL's Coach of the Year.

Davis also made a quick impression on the AFL's team owners. The new league was having a hard time competing with the long-established NFL, so the owners named him AFL commissioner in 1966, and he relocated to New York to try to improve the AFL's fortunes. After hiring head coach John Rauch to lead the Raiders, Davis launched a campaign against the NFL by signing many of its stars to AFL contracts. (Davis's aggressive work set in motion an NFL–AFL merger that would be completed in 1970. Because Davis himself was against the merger, the NFL would be kept to two conferences—the National Football Conference [NFC] and the American Football Conference [AFC]—as a compromise.)

Davis returned to Oakland late in 1966 after his brief commissionership was completed, and he immediately shook up the roster in search of talent that could complement stalwart players such as wide receiver Fred Biletnikoff. He traded for cornerback Willie Brown and young quarterback Daryle "The Mad

Branding the Raiders

When the Oakland Raiders franchise was founded in 1960, the team had trouble getting off the ground. With black, gold, and white hand-me-down uniforms, no helmet logo, and a 9–33 record over its first three seasons, the team had a horrible image. So when Al Davis took over, his first order of business was to forge the Raiders brand. And he started with the logo—a shield with crossed swords and a "raider," or pirate, wearing an old-time football helmet. "We all believe in the patch [logo]," Davis said. "Just like Disney says 'Mickey Mouse [is the symbol] of the entertainment world,' I believe this is the patch of the sports world. I believe the Raiders are global." Davis also trademarked his team's slogans: "Pride and Poise," "Commitment to Excellence," and "Just Win, Baby" in an all-out effort to get the Raiders into the public consciousness. But Davis knew none of it would work without on-field success, and the Raiders soon had that, becoming a powerhouse in the 1970s. "What's important is winning," he said. "In my culture, in our culture, in the Raider Culture."

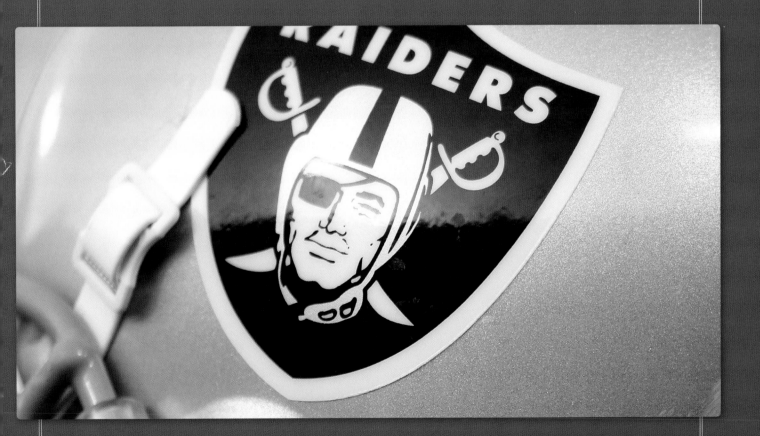

THE ICONIC PIRATE LOGO ADORNS THE RAIDERS' SILVER HELMETS

OFFENSIVE LINEMEN ART SHELL, GENE UPSHAW, AND HENRY LAWRENCE IN 1977

Bomber" Lamonica, drafted guard Gene Upshaw, and took a chance on veteran quarterback George Blanda. By the start of the 1967 season, Oakland had a strong team with intriguing potential.

Oakland surged to 13–1 that season behind Lamonica's 30 touchdown passes. After dominating the Houston Oilers 40–7 in the AFL Championship Game, the Raiders marched into Super Bowl II to face legendary coach Vince Lombardi and his NFL champion Green Bay Packers. Lamonica and scoring-machine tight end Billy Cannon did their best, but it wasn't enough, and the Raiders lost 33–14. Nevertheless, the Raiders had served notice. They were now a force with which to be reckoned.

Al Davis

TEAM OWNER / RAIDERS SEASONS: 1963–2011

Al Davis never played a single down of professional football. But after taking over the Oakland Raiders in 1963, he became the living embodiment of the franchise. To him, image and style were just as important as winning, and his devotion to the "Silver and Black" was all-consuming. This was reflected even in his wardrobe, which was made up almost entirely of black, white, and silver warm-up suits (and not just because he was colorblind). Davis almost always wore a Super Bowl ring on each hand, dark sunglasses, and a slicked-back hairstyle—a look that reinforced the maverick image that he always preferred. "His life is the Raiders," explained former special teams coach Steve Ortmayer. "That's not a statement to be taken lightly, like a lot of people's life is what they do. It's to an extent he has never taken a day off from the Raiders. Never." Davis was the only person in the NFL ever to have served in six different positions— player personnel assistant, assistant coach, head coach, general manager, league commissioner, and the principal owner of a team. He played an active role in the organization until his death in 2011.

The Greatest Comeback Never Seen

On November 17, 1968, Oakland played the New York Jets in a matchup that featured two of the AFL's marquee teams and 10 future Hall-of-Famers. But that's not why it was voted the 10th Most Memorable Game of the Century by fans on NFL.com. Rather, it's because Oakland's stunning comeback win was seen by few fans. Following the 4:00 P.M. game, the NBC television network was set to air the movie *Heidi*, based on the popular children's book, at 7:00 P.M. So when New York took a 32–29 lead with just over a minute remaining, NBC figured the game was effectively over and switched to *Heidi* everywhere except on the West Coast. Viewers who had hoped to see the end of the game were disappointed— but not as disappointed as when they found out the Raiders had scored two late touchdowns to win 43–32. NBC was so bombarded by complaints that the network was forced to issue a public apology. "Probably the most significant factor to come out of *Heidi* was, whatever you do, you better not leave an NFL football game," said Val Pinchbeck, the NFL's former chief of broadcasting.

Madden Makes a Winner

After Oakland lost to the New York Jets in the 1968 AFL Championship Game, Coach Rauch took the Buffalo Bills' head coaching job. So, in 1969, Davis handed the head-coaching reins to linebackers coach John Madden, who immediately instilled a different attitude in the locker room. "I had a philosophy," Madden explained. "I really liked my players. I liked them as people. I made a point to talk to each player personally every day.... You can be intense and competitive and all that, but try to remember to laugh and have fun. It's just a football game."

The Raiders went 12–1–1 under their rookie head coach and drubbed the Oilers 56–7 in the playoffs before being ousted 17–7 by the rival Kansas City Chiefs in the next round. With a Lamonica and Blanda quarterback tandem, Oakland won the new AFC West Division title in 1970 and reached

THE RAIDERS THRIVED WITH JOHN MADDEN AND DARYLE LAMONICA MAKING THE CALLS

Fred Biletnikoff

WIDE RECEIVER / RAIDERS SEASONS: 1965–78 / HEIGHT: 6-FOOT-1 / WEIGHT: 190 POUNDS

Al Davis always preferred a vertical passing offense—in other words, quarterbacks with powerful arms and speedy receivers that could catch long bombs downfield. But he made an exception for slow-footed Fred Biletnikoff. "We felt, with our approach to total pass offense, that speed wasn't the only consideration," Davis said. In Biletnikoff, the Raiders got a tough, hard-nosed, go-to receiver who was not afraid of running across the middle of the field where linebackers might crush him. A precise route-runner with superb hand-eye coordination, Biletnikoff was known as a player who could catch even the worst passes. "The guy can catch anything he can touch," Raiders coach John Madden said. "That's no accident. Some receivers might catch 15 passes in practice. Fred will stick around and catch 100." Biletnikoff excelled every Sunday, but he seemed to find an extra gear in the playoffs. In 19 postseason games, he set NFL records with 70 catches, 1,167 yards, and 10 touchdowns. As a testament to his longevity, Biletnikoff caught 40 or more passes in 10 consecutive seasons. He was inducted into the Pro Football Hall of Fame in 1988.

"The guy can catch anything he can touch."

JOHN MADDEN ON FRED BILETNIKOFF

the AFC Championship Game against the Baltimore Colts. The game started close, but after Blanda threw two late end-zone interceptions, the Colts prevailed, 27–17.

After a second straight 8–4–2 record in 1971, the Raiders improved to 10–3–1 in 1972. In a playoff game that year against the Pittsburgh Steelers, the Raiders had all but won when a routine collision turned into an improbable loss. Backup quarterback Ken Stabler replaced an ill Lamonica at the start of the fourth quarter and showed fans why he was nicknamed "The Snake" when he scrambled for a 30-yard score to stake Oakland to a 7–6 lead. Then, on 4th-down-and-10 with 22 seconds left, Steelers quarterback Terry Bradshaw threw the deflected touchdown pass that became known as the "Immaculate Reception," and Oakland was left stunned by a 13–7 loss.

The next year, Coach Madden named Stabler his starter—a position the gritty southpaw would hold for the rest of the 1970s. During those years, Oakland also became known for its fearsome defense. Safety Jack Tatum was nicknamed "The Assassin" for his frighteningly fierce tackles; Ted Hendricks was a versatile, 6-foot-7 linebacker nicknamed the "Mad Stork"; and cornerback Willie Brown didn't need a nickname to become the club's all-time interceptions leader (with 39).

With this impressive lineup, the "Silver and Black" reached the AFC Championship Game in 1973, 1974, and 1975—and lost every time. To make matters worse, each opponent went on to win the Super Bowl. By 1976, the Raiders had a reputation as a team that couldn't win the big one.

Deceptive Reception

If there's one play throughout history that angers the Oakland Raiders the most, it's the one that most people know as the "Immaculate Reception." In the final seconds of a 1972 playoff game, Raiders safety Jack Tatum went to break up a pass to the Pittsburgh Steelers' Frenchy Fuqua, drilling Fuqua and popping the ball in the air. When Fuqua's trailing teammate, Franco Harris, caught it and scored a touchdown, Raiders defenders assumed that Fuqua had hit the ball to Harris—an illegal play at the time—so the play should have been ruled incomplete. However, no official had a clear view of the play, so referee Fred Swearingen spoke with Art McNally, the NFL's supervisor of officials. At the time, instant replay was not used by NFL officials. However, it is believed that McNally viewed the play on a television screen in the press box, after which Swearingen called it a touchdown. "It remains the most incredible, implausible finish to a football game," Oakland center Jim Otto said. "It also was the birth of television instant replay." To this day, many Raiders players on that 1972 team maintain that Pittsburgh won on an illegal play.

REMEMBERING THE "IMMACULATE RECEPTION" STILL STINGS IN OAKLAND

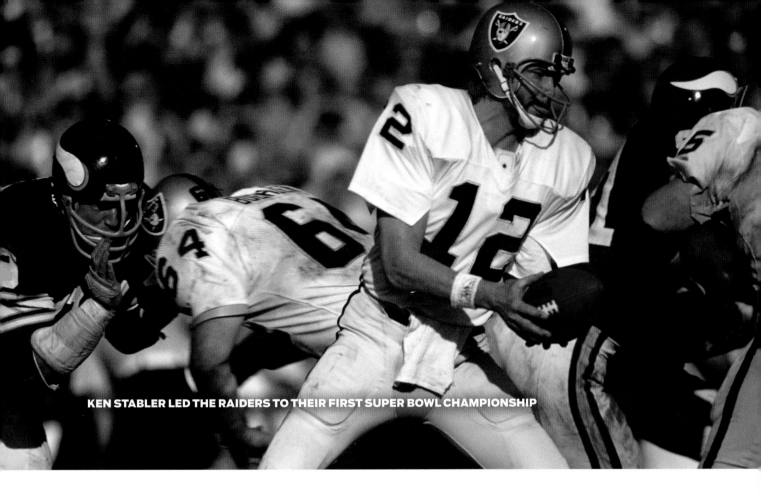

KEN STABLER LED THE RAIDERS TO THEIR FIRST SUPER BOWL CHAMPIONSHIP

But Davis refused to give up on Madden, and Madden refused to give up on his players. With Stabler tossing 27 touchdown passes and the defense stronger than ever, Oakland went 13–1 in 1976. Its only stumble was a lopsided 48–17 loss to the New England Patriots. In the playoffs, the Raiders exacted revenge on the Patriots with a dramatic, 24–21 victory that entailed two fourth-quarter Oakland touchdowns. After demolishing Pittsburgh 24–7 in the AFC Championship Game, the Raiders faced the Minnesota Vikings in Super Bowl XI.

On Super Bowl Sunday, tackle Art Shell and guard Gene Upshaw made the left side of the Raiders' offensive line dominant. This road-grading tandem manhandled Pro Bowl defensive linemen Alan Page and Jim Marshall, part of Minnesota's vaunted "Purple People Eaters" line. They blew open holes for van Eeghen and halfback Clarence Davis as the Raiders ran for 266 yards on a whopping 52 carries for a 32–14 victory and their first world championship. Biletnikoff was named the game's Most Valuable Player (MVP), but the conquest was truly a team effort.

The Raiders came back strong in 1977 with an 11–3 record, but they were shaky in the playoffs. In the first round against the Baltimore Colts, Raiders kicker Errol Mann sent the contest into overtime with a game-tying field goal. After a scoreless first overtime, Stabler finally hit tight end Dave Casper for the winning score in the second overtime. Although the AFC Championship Game versus the Denver Broncos was a tight affair, Stabler threw an interception that contributed to a 20–17 Oakland loss.

JIM PLUNKETT REVIVED HIS CAREER AND WON A TITLE WITH THE RAIDERS

The Raiders went 9–7 in each of the next two seasons and missed the playoffs, and then Madden retired in 1979 to pursue a broadcasting career. But what a decade it had been—Oakland won the AFC West six times, made the playoffs seven times, and earned a lasting reputation as a team willing to sign troublemakers, outcasts, and aging stars and mold them into winners.

Under new coach Tom Flores, a former Raiders quarterback, Oakland went 11–5 in 1980. The two players most responsible for this success were cornerback Lester Hayes and quarterback Jim Plunkett. Hayes picked off an incredible 13 interceptions during the season and 5 more in the playoffs. Plunkett was a veteran backup whose NFL career had seemed finished when he joined Oakland in 1978. After Oakland lost three of its first five games in 1980, and starting quarterback Dan Pastorini went down with a broken leg, Flores called on Plunkett, who guided the Raiders to 9 wins in their next 11 games. After winning three playoff games, Oakland became the first Wild Card team ever to reach the Super Bowl.

Few experts gave the Raiders a chance against the powerful Philadelphia Eagles, but Oakland had already beaten the odds. Completing both the Raiders' incredible comeback and his own, Plunkett tossed a Super Bowl–record 80-yard touchdown pass to fullback Kenny King on Oakland's second possession. Plunkett's 261 passing yards and 3 touchdown passes propelled Oakland to a 27–10 win and earned him MVP honors.

Ghostly Plays

Oakland tight end Dave "The Ghost" Casper was responsible for not one, not two, but three historic plays. The first two came in a 1977 AFC playoff game against the Baltimore Colts. Casper's "Ghost to the Post" play, in which he ran downfield toward the goalpost, resulted in a 42-yard reception that set up a game-tying field goal to force overtime. Then, in the second overtime, he caught a 10-yard, game-winning touchdown. Early the next season, he helped complete a play that became known as "The Holy Roller." Oakland was trailing the San Diego Chargers 20–14 on the last play of the game when quarterback Ken Stabler intentionally fumbled, and Raiders running back Pete Banaszak batted the ball toward the goal line. Casper then awkwardly fell on it in the end zone to score the game-winning touchdown. "It would've been nicer to do it a little smoother," Casper joked, "with a little more skill and like a dancer or something." The famous play brought about an NFL rule change; beginning the next season, only the initial fumbler could legally advance the ball on fourth down or inside the final two minutes of a half.

DAVE CASPER'S LAST NAME INSPIRED HIS SUPERNATURAL NICKNAME

LYLE ALZADO BOLSTERED THE RAIDERS' DEFENSE DURING THE EARLY '80s

Raiding L.A.

In 1981, the Raiders uncharacteristically lost three straight shutouts early on and limped to a 7–9 record. Then, before a 1982 season that was shortened by a players' strike, Davis relocated the Raiders to Los Angeles to capitalize on the franchise's popularity in the larger Southern California market.

The Raiders' transition to "L.A." was made easier with the drafting of Marcus Allen, a fast and shifty running back who had just won the Heisman Trophy as college football's best player at the local University of Southern California. Allen rushed for 697 yards, caught passes for 401 more, and scored 14 total touchdowns to win the NFL Offensive Rookie of the Year award.

The Raiders' defense also got a makeover when defensive end Howie Long forced his way into the starting lineup and the team signed Cleveland Browns defensive tackle Lyle "Darth Raider" Alzado. Boosted, too, by fleet-footed linebacker Rod Martin, the rugged "D" quickly won new L.A. fans over.

In 1983, the Raiders went 12–4 and returned to the Super Bowl, which Allen turned

THE VERSATILE MARCUS ALLEN CARRIED THE RAIDERS TO SUPER BOWL GLORY

John Madden

COACH / RAIDERS SEASONS: 1969—78

As a junior offensive lineman at California Polytechnic State University in 1958, John Madden was drafted by the Philadelphia Eagles. But his playing career ended before it started when he injured his knee in training camp his rookie year. The injury turned out to be a blessing in disguise. Madden would arrive early before practice to get treatment, only to find Eagles quarterback Norm Van Brocklin watching game films. Eventually, Van Brocklin asked Madden to assist him with play breakdowns. "I learned more about football than ever before," Madden said. "Van Brocklin was a bright guy, and he taught me all about the passing game and how to attack a defense." Once he learned his injury was career-ending, the genial, talkative Madden decided to become a coach. He took over as head coach of the Raiders in 1969 and held the position for a decade. Under his stewardship, Oakland never suffered a losing season. Following his coaching tenure, Madden became a successful broadcaster and earned fame for his custom-made Madden Cruiser bus, his annual "All-Madden" teams, and his popular *Madden NFL* video game franchise.

MANY CONSIDER RAY GUY TO BE THE GREATEST PUNTER IN NFL HISTORY

into his own personal showcase, with 191 rushing yards and 2 touchdowns—including a sensational 74-yard scoring run. The Raiders trounced the Washington Redskins 38–9 for their third world title. Although Allen would remain a Raiders star for many seasons, few performances would match Super Bowl XVIII's. "This has to be the greatest feeling of my life," he said. "I've been to the Rose Bowl. I've won the Heisman Trophy. But nothing is sweeter than this."

The Raiders compiled winning records over the next two seasons but were bounced in the first round of the playoffs each time. Even though Los Angeles featured a number of exceptional players—including tight end Todd Christensen and cornerback Mike Haynes—by 1987, things were getting ugly. Flores and preeminent punter Ray Guy both retired. Then the team's new coach, Mike Shanahan, clashed with Davis's overbearing personality and would last fewer than two seasons.

But the excitement level rose with the arrival of another Heisman Trophy winner: running back Vincent

"Bo" Jackson. He featured an uncanny combination of speed and strength and, along with Allen, gave Los Angeles a potent one-two punch at running back.

Still, the Raiders needed more talent at other positions. And they found some in the form of Tim Brown from the University of Notre Dame. The first wide receiver ever to win the Heisman Trophy, Brown's prowess as a kick returner made him a dangerous weapon. Although Jackson and Brown racked up some impressive statistics, wins were still in short supply in Los Angeles.

Looking to stabilize the team, Davis hired former star Art Shell as head coach in 1989. Shell patiently coached according to Raiders tradition, emphasizing a strong passing offense and a stout defense. He relied on

What Could Have Been

Few players in NFL history had the potential of Vincent "Bo" Jackson. A physical anomaly, Jackson was a halfback who had the bulk of a fullback and the speed of a wide receiver. In fact, as of 2013, Jackson had the fastest official 40-yard dash time—4.12 seconds—of any NFL player ever recorded. His flashes of brilliance included a 221-yard, 3-touchdown performance in which he sprinted 91 yards for one score and bowled over much-hyped Seattle Seahawks linebacker Brian Bosworth for another. Still, Bo's true potential was never realized. During his NFL career, Jackson also played professional baseball for the Kansas City Royals, causing him to miss the first five or six games of each football season. And when he was in football pads, he shared carries with Hall-of-Famer Marcus Allen. Worst of all, Jackson suffered a hip injury in the 1990 playoffs that ended his promising NFL career after just four seasons. Decades later, Jackson is still remembered as an almost unstoppable player on the classic video game *Tecmo Bowl* and for the Nike "Bo Knows" advertising campaign, which emphasized that Jackson excelled at virtually anything he tried.

BEFORE SUFFERING A HIP INJURY, BO JACKSON THRILLED FANS THROUGHOUT THE NFL

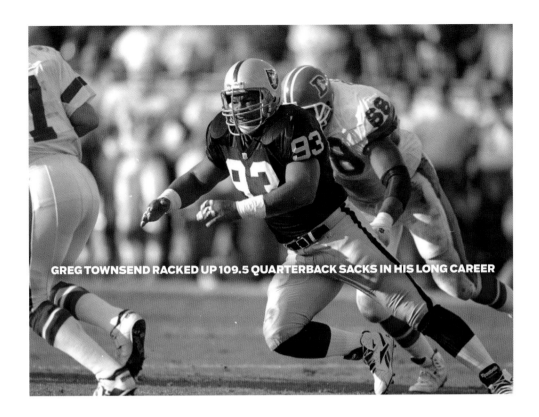

GREG TOWNSEND RACKED UP 109.5 QUARTERBACK SACKS IN HIS LONG CAREER

leaders such as standout guard Steve Wisniewski to help solidify the offense, while defensive end Greg Townsend and cornerback Terry McDaniel galvanized the defense. These players led the Raiders to some solid seasons in the early '90s, including postseason appearances in 1990 and 1991.

nfortunately for Raiders fans, Jackson's bright career ended when he injured his hip in a 20–10 playoff win over the Cincinnati Bengals after the 1990 season. The Raiders were then trounced 51–3 by the Buffalo Bills in the AFC Championship Game. Success was harder to come by the next few years, as the Raiders either missed the playoffs or lost in the early rounds.

After some ups and downs in Los Angeles, Davis decided to move his franchise back to Oakland in 1995, much to the delight of Oakland's still passionate fan base, whose devoted allegiance earned them the title "Raider Nation." Despite the Raiders' middling 8–8 record that season, "The Black Hole" (Oakland Coliseum's seating section for the most enthusiastic fans) was a raucous place once again.

JON GRUDEN WAS CALLED "CHUCKY" AFTER A CHARACTER IN A 1988 MOVIE

Trying to Right the Ship

In 1998, after the Raiders endured back-to-back losing seasons, Davis hired 34-year-old Jon Gruden as head coach. Gruden was younger than some of his players, but this may have actually worked to his advantage. His fiery demeanor and competitiveness seemed contagious, and young players such as cornerback Charles Woodson mirrored Gruden's desire to win.

To complement the young talent and provide on-field leadership, veteran quarterback Rich Gannon was added to the roster in 1999. After going 8–8 that season, the Raiders jumped to 12–4 in 2000. Oakland then shut out the Miami Dolphins 27–0 in the playoffs but hit a roadblock in the AFC Championship Game, losing 16–3 to the Baltimore Ravens, who went on to win the Super Bowl.

The next year, Oakland went 10–6 before battling the New England Patriots in a snowy playoff game that has become known as the "Tuck Rule Game." The Raiders

CHARLES WOODSON SPENT THE FIRST HALF OF HIS STELLAR CAREER IN OAKLAND

TACKLE ROBERT GALLERY WAS THE SECOND OVERALL PICK IN THE 2004 DRAFT

Howie Long

If it hadn't been for Oakland defensive line coach Earl Leggett, Howie Long might not have worn a Raiders jersey or built a Hall of Fame career that included eight Pro Bowls. "Nobody was really after him [in the 1981 NFL Draft]," Leggett said. "But I didn't want to take a chance. I was pushing him real hard on draft day." After the Raiders drafted him, Long became Leggett's personal project in training camp. "Every day at practice, it was a new position," Long said. "I couldn't understand what he was doing at the time." What Leggett was doing was taking advantage of Long's strength, quickness, and intense desire to excel. And he helped turn Long into one of the most versatile linemen in the league. Although he consistently ranked near the top of the NFL in sack totals, Long played the run just as well. "There are guys who are bigger, guys who are stronger, guys who are meaner," said teammate Matt Millen, a linebacker. "But none of them puts it together the way he does. Nobody has his blend. He does everything." After retiring, Long became a highly regarded NFL television analyst.

appeared to seal a 13–10 victory late in the fourth quarter when Woodson sacked Patriots quarterback Tom Brady and forced a fumble that the Raiders recovered. However, the play was reviewed and overturned, with the referee stating that Brady's arm was moving forward and that the fumble was, therefore, technically an incomplete pass. Patriots kicker Adam Vinatieri kicked a 45-yard field goal to send the game into overtime. He then kicked another to bury Oakland's Super Bowl hopes.

Despite Gruden's impressive winning percentage, the opinionated Davis did not agree with how he was running the team and made the unusual decision to trade Gruden to the Tampa Bay Buccaneers for cash and four draft picks. Although many

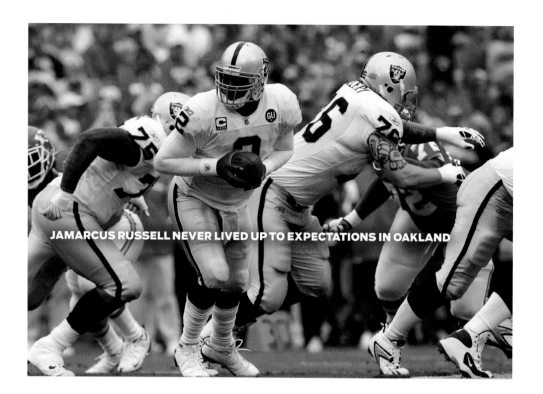

JAMARCUS RUSSELL NEVER LIVED UP TO EXPECTATIONS IN OAKLAND

fans and players were sorry to see Gruden leave, the 2002 Raiders came back stronger than ever under new coach Bill Callahan. Gannon had the finest season of his career, passing for 4,689 yards and 26 touchdowns to win the NFL MVP award—an especially remarkable feat, considering it came in the 15th season of a career in which he was often a backup.

The Raiders handily won two playoff games to reach the Super Bowl for the first time in 19 years. There they faced former coach Gruden and the Buccaneers. "There is going to be a natural rivalry in this Super Bowl, and that's not all bad," Raiders defensive end Trace Armstrong said. "I thought he [Gruden] was an excellent coach.... But that doesn't mean we don't want to beat him." Unfortunately for Oakland, Gruden didn't pull any punches, either, and his Bucs scored three defensive touchdowns as they demolished Oakland 48–21.

That defeat seemed to send the Raiders into a tailspin, as they would suffer losing records the next seven seasons. Along the way, Oakland claimed the undesirable title of most penalized team in the NFL, went through five head coaches, and drafted booming kicker Sebastian Janikowski.

The biggest changes in Oakland began in 2007. Davis shook up the franchise and made headlines when he hired 31-year-old Lane Kiffin as the youngest head coach in the history of the NFL. Then Oakland selected enormous Louisiana State University quarterback JaMarcus Russell with the top overall

The Black Hole

Affectionately referred to as "Raider Nation," fans of the Oakland Raiders are some of the most unusual and passionate in all of professional sports. "We are Raider fans," wrote fan/author Craig Parker. "We pretend to know who these guys [players] are. They're the Silver-and-Black Gang. And they will gang tackle as soon as look at you. And we know what they're after. They want an AFC West Division title with home-field advantage throughout the playoffs." The most fanatical members of Raider Nation are known for occupying "The Black Hole," which encompasses seating sections 104, 105, 106, and 107 of the O.co Coliseum. The spot is frequented by arguably the rowdiest and most colorful fans in the league. Some dress up in ornate costumes that make them look like futuristic football warriors, complete with black-and-silver makeup, war helmets, and spiked shoulder pads. "It's amazing," Raiders tight end Rickey Dudley said. "You know why they call it the Raider Nation? Because it's nationwide. Miami, New York, wherever. You're part of the Raider Nation. It's so large. They say Dallas is America's Team. Well, I'm not so sure about that. The Raiders are beloved."

"THE BLACK HOLE" REPRESENTS THE HEART OF RAIDER NATION

DEFENSIVE END DERRICK BURGESS MADE LIFE DIFFICULT FOR OPPOSING QUARTERBACKS

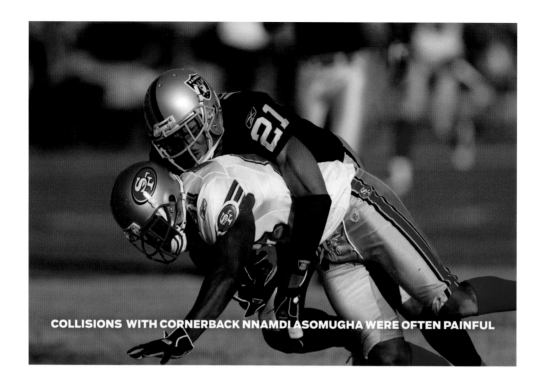

COLLISIONS WITH CORNERBACK NNAMDI ASOMUGHA WERE OFTEN PAINFUL

pick in the NFL Draft. Despite these shakeups, the 2007 Raiders still went just 4–12.

After starting the next season 1–3, Davis made headlines again by firing Kiffin. Russell's Oakland days were also numbered, as his play progressively worsened and he struggled with off-field issues, including substance abuse problems and a poor work ethic. After the Raiders lost 11 games in both 2008 and 2009, Russell was cut.

The 2010 Raiders returned to respectability with an 8–8 record, thanks in part to the play of speedy halfback Darren McFadden and sure-tackling safety Tyvon Branch. The early weeks of the 2011 campaign brought mixed emotions to Raiders fans. Oakland got off to a promising 4–2 start, but around the same time, Davis, the longtime face of the franchise, passed away at the age of 82. Controversy then arose when the club traded away high future draft selections for quarterback Carson Palmer, who, in six seasons as the starter in Cincinnati, had never won a playoff game.

Despite McFadden suffering a season-ending foot injury in Week 7, the Raiders were in position to reach the playoffs for the first time in nine years if they could win their final game of the season against the division rival San Diego Chargers. Palmer threw for 417 yards and 2 touchdowns, but Oakland gave up 38 points in a disappointing loss. In the aftermath, Dennis Allen was hired as the Raiders' new head coach and expressed optimism for Oakland's future. "I don't think radical changes are what need to be made," the coach said. "I feel like we've got enough players, both on offense and defense, that we can win a championship with."

Tim Brown

WIDE RECEIVER / RAIDERS SEASONS: 1988–2003 / HEIGHT: 6 FEET / WEIGHT: 195 POUNDS

Throughout his entire 16-year career with the Raiders, "Touchdown Timmy" Brown remained a consistent star. The first wide receiver ever to win the prestigious Heisman Trophy, Brown made an immediate impact in his rookie season. He led the NFL in kickoff returns, and combining those yards with his punt return, receiving, and even rushing gains, Brown amassed a total of 2,317 yards, which remains an NFL rookie record. The self-proclaimed "Mr. Raider" holds most of the team's receiving records, and his 240 games played and 9 Pro Bowl appearances wearing the Silver and Black are the most in franchise history. Brown never ceased to amaze teammates and coaches with his great instincts and ability to learn new offensive plays. "We call him 'The Natural,'" coach Jon Gruden said. "You tell him one time, you show him one time, and you can expect perfection." Ever the perfectionist, Brown decided to leave the team in 2003 rather than accept a reduced role on the offense. "When you've played at the level I've played at," Brown explained, "it's tough to sit on the sidelines waving a towel."

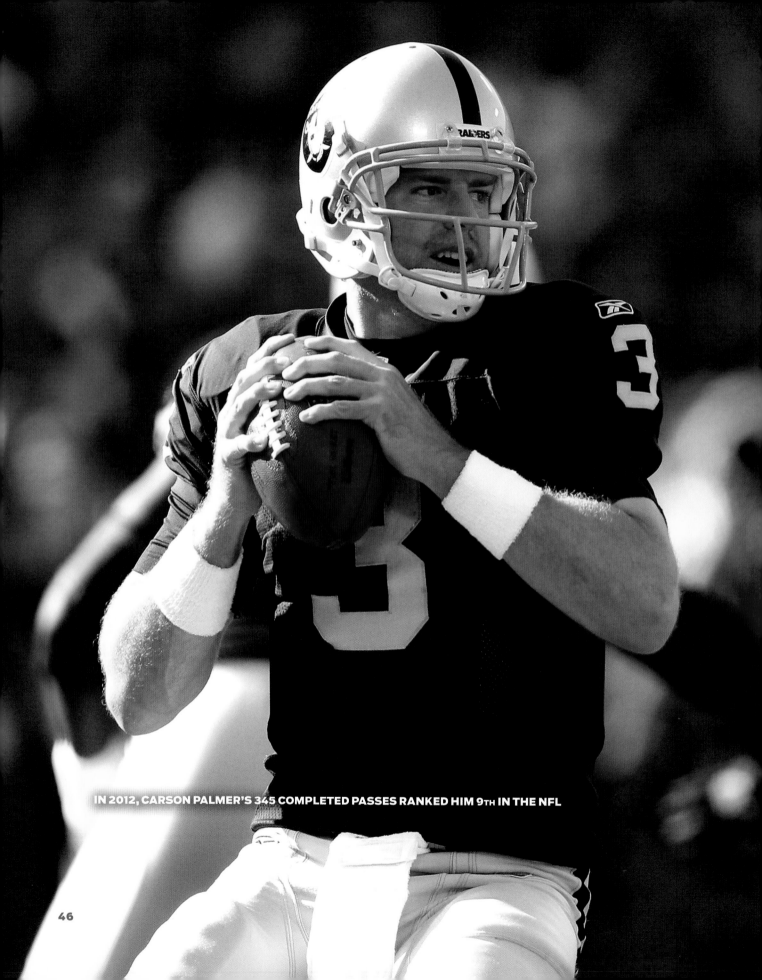

IN 2012, CARSON PALMER'S 345 COMPLETED PASSES RANKED HIM 9TH IN THE NFL

DEFENDERS (L-R) TYVON BRANCH, DESMOND BRYANT, AND TOMMY KELLY

Allen's optimism came in handy when the 2012 NFL Draft began and Oakland could not choose any new players until the third round. Throughout the season that followed, the Raiders were hit with a rash of injuries, especially to key players, and lacked depth overall. After opening the 2012 season 3–4, the team won just one game the rest of the way to finish 4–12. It was Oakland's 10th straight year with a losing record. But there were signs that things could turn around. Palmer threw for more than 4,000 yards despite the injuries suffered by his receiving corps. His favorite target was tight end Brandon Myers, who shattered his previous season's career-best 16 catches by hauling in 79 tosses and averaging more than 10 yards per reception. Additionally, wideout Rod Streator had the fourth-most catches by a rookie in Raiders history.

The history of the Oakland Raiders is one of the NFL's great stories. From their quirky beginning, to their eccentric longtime owner, to their relocation and "unrelocation," to their alternating eras of domination and futility, no organization is quite like the Raiders. Author Mark Ribowsky once wrote that the team was a group of "odds and ends, oddities and irregulars, factory seconds and seeming chain-gang escapees." It's an image the team's players are proud of and will continue to wear as a badge of honor as they chase their next world championship.

INDEX